W9-BEY-529

Harry Houdini

Illusionist & Stunt Performer

by Grace Hansen

Abdo
HISTORY MAKER
BIOGRAPHIES
Kids

abdopublishing.com

Published by Abdo Kids, a division of ABDO, PO Box 398166, Minneapolis, Minnesota 55439.

Printed in the United States of America, North Mankato, Minnesota.

102015

012016

THIS BOOK CONTAINS RECYCLED MATERIALS

Photo Credits: Corbis, Getty Images, iStock, Library of Congress, Shutterstock, ©Harvard Theatre Collection, Houghton Library p.5, ©User:rcade / CC-SA-2.0 p.7

Production Contributors: Teddy Borth, Jennie Forsberg, Grace Hansen

Design Contributors: Laura Mitchell, Dorothy Toth

Library of Congress Control Number: 2015941769

Cataloging-in-Publication Data

Hansen, Grace.

 Harry Houdini: illusionist & stunt performer / Grace Hansen.

  p. cm. -- (History maker biographies)

Includes index.

ISBN 978-1-68080-125-5

1. Houdini, Harry, 1874-1926--Juvenile literature. 2. Magicians--United States--Biography--Juvenile literature. 3. Escape artists--United States--Biography--Juvenile literature. 1. Title.

793.8/092--dc23

[B]

                    2015941769

Table of Contents

Birth

Erik Weisz was born on March 24, 1874. He was born in Budapest, Hungary. In 1878, his family left for the United States. They settled in Appleton, Wisconsin.

EUROPE

ASIA

Hungary

AFRICA

5

The Magic Begins

In 1887, the family moved to New York City, New York. Later, Erik and his friend Jacob started a magic act. They called themselves "The Brothers Houdini." Erik went by Harry Houdini.

In 1893, Jacob left the act. Harry met a girl named Bess. The two married. Bess also joined the act. Together, they were "The Houdinis."

In 1899, Houdini performed his handcuff act in St. Paul, MN. A theater manager was watching. He set the Houdinis up for shows around the country.

In 1907, Harry performed his bridge jump. Cuffed and chained, he jumped into water. He freed himself and swam to the **surface**. It was unsafe. But people believed they had seen magic.

In 1912, Harry **debuted** the

underwater box escape.

By 1918, he had perfected

another trick. He made an

elephant disappear!

Hollywood

Harry's **popularity** caught Hollywood's attention. He starred in his first motion picture in 1918. It was called *The Master Mystery*.

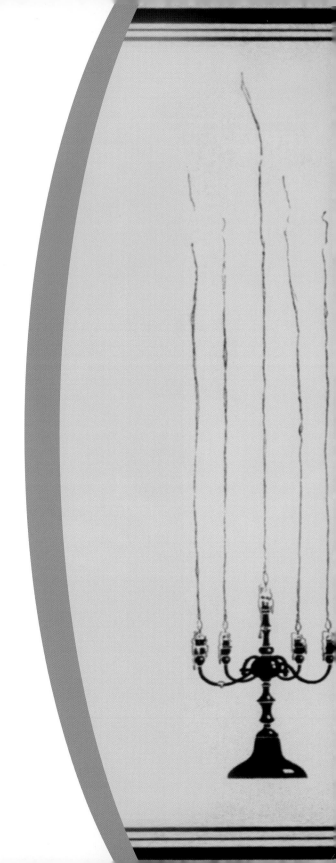

B. A. ROLFE PRODUCTIONS

OCTAGON FILMS, INC.

HOUDINI

IN

The Master Mystery

A Super - Serial in Fifteen Episodes

EPISODE TWELVE

"The Death Noose"

B. A. ROLFE PRODUCTIONS

17

Harry did many **stunts** in his movies. People loved it. Now he was known for more than just magic.

19

Death & Legacy

In 1926, Harry died on Halloween in Detroit, MI. He is remembered as a great entertainer.

Timeline

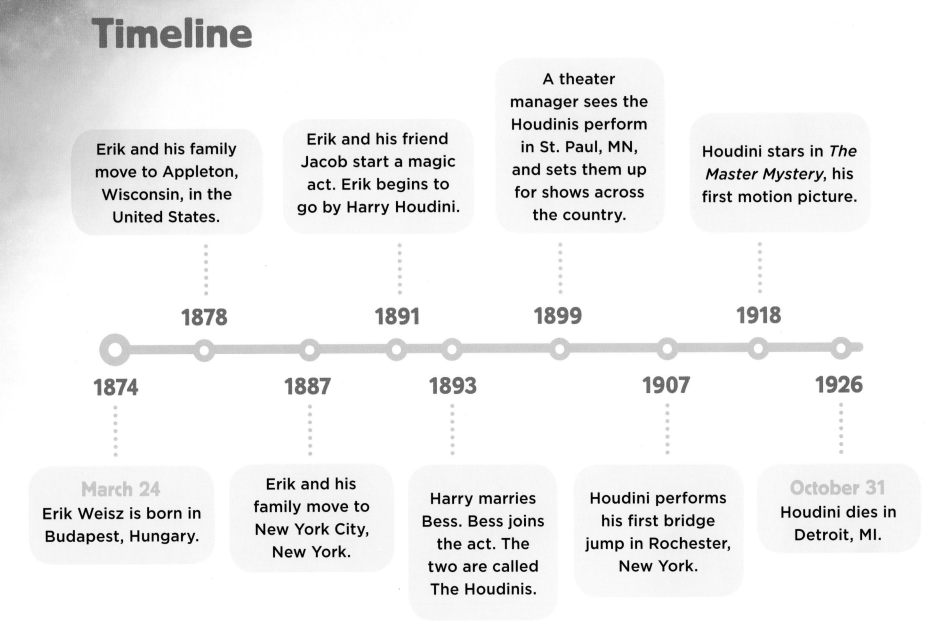

Erik and his family move to Appleton, Wisconsin, in the United States.

Erik and his friend Jacob start a magic act. Erik begins to go by Harry Houdini.

A theater manager sees the Houdinis perform in St. Paul, MN, and sets them up for shows across the country.

Houdini stars in *The Master Mystery*, his first motion picture.

1878

1891

1899

1918

1874

1887

1893

1907

1926

March 24
Erik Weisz is born in Budapest, Hungary.

Erik and his family move to New York City, New York.

Harry marries Bess. Bess joins the act. The two are called The Houdinis.

Houdini performs his first bridge jump in Rochester, New York.

October 31
Houdini dies in Detroit, MI.

Glossary

debut – the first public appearance.

popularity – the favor of the general public.

stunt – a performance showing a person's athletic skill.

surface – just above water.

Index

abdokids.com

Use this code to log on to abdokids.com and access crafts, games, videos, and more!

Abdo Kids Code:
HHK1255